The Ultima Zealand Travel Guide 2023

Journey to the land of Middle-earth and discover the magic of New Zealand like a citizen

By

Robyn Russel

Copyright

Except for brief quotations incorporated in critical reviews and certain other noncommercial uses permitted by copyright law, no part of this publication may be reproduced, distributed, or transmitted in any form or by any means, including photocopying, recording, or other electronic or mechanical methods, without the publisher's prior written permission.

The Ultimate New Zealand Travel Guide 2023:

Journey to the land of Middle-earth and discover the magic of New Zealand like a citizen

All rights reserved.

Copyright ©2022 Robyn Russel

Robyn Russel

Copyright 1

Introduction.. 7

Chapter 1: General information about New Zealand 11

    The geography and climate of New Zealand 14

Chapter 2: Planning your trip to New Zealand 17

    How to get there 18

    Visa requirements 20

    Where to stay 21

    What to pack 23

Chapter 3: The North Island: Cities, culture, and adventure 27

    The major cities of the North Island 27

    Cultural attractions and events 28

Chapter 4: The South Island: Natural beauty and outdoor activities 31

    The major cities of the South Island 31

    Natural attractions and national parks 33

    Outdoor activities and adventure sports 35

Chapter 5: Maori culture and traditions 39

    The history and culture of the Maori people 39

Traditional Maori arts and crafts --------------------------------------- 40

Maori cultural experiences and performances-------------------------- 42

Chapter 6: The best food and drink in New Zealand ---------------- 45

Traditional Maori cuisine -- 48

Regional specialties and local delicacies ---------------------------------- 51

The best places to eat and drink in New Zealand ---------------------- 53

Chapter 7: The most iconic film locations in New Zealand ------- 57

The Lord of the Rings film locations in New Zealand ------------------ 62

Chapter 8: Must-see landmarks and hidden gems ----------------- 69

Secret spots and hidden gems off the beaten track -------------------- 74

Insider tips for experiencing the best of New Zealand---------------- 76

Chapter 9: Tips for traveling like a local in New Zealand --------- 81

The best time of year to visit-- 85

How to get around the country -- 87

Local customs and etiquette -- 89

Where to find the best deals and discounts ---------------------------- 93

Chapter 10: Why New Zealand is a must-visit destination ------- 97

The many reasons to visit New Zealand ---------------------------------- 99

How to make the most of your trip to New Zealand ------------------ 104

Tips for traveling with kids or pets -------------------------------------- **109**

Conclusion-- ***113***

Robyn Russel

The Ultimate New Zealand

Travel Guide 2023

Introduction

As a Lover of New Zealand, I am constantly amazed by the incredible beauty and diversity of the country. From the bustling cities of Auckland and Wellington to the tranquil countryside and stunning natural landscapes, there is always something new to discover and explore in New Zealand.

One of the things I love most about New Zealand is the outdoor activities and adventure sports that are available here. Whether you're a thrill-seeker looking to bungee jump or skydive, or a nature lover who wants to hike or bike through the stunning national parks, there's something for everyone in New Zealand.

But it's not just the adventure and outdoor activities that make New Zealand special - it's also the unique culture and traditions of the Maori people, who have called this land home for thousands of years. From traditional Maori arts and crafts to cultural experiences and performances, there are many ways to learn about and experience Maori culture in New Zealand.

And of course, no trip to New Zealand would be complete without experiencing the delicious food and drink that the country has to offer. From traditional Maori cuisine to regional specialties and local delicacies, there's something for every palate in New Zealand.

But perhaps the thing that sets New Zealand apart from other destinations is its association with the world-famous Lord of the Rings films. Many of the iconic locations from the films can be found right here in New Zealand, and it's truly magical to visit these places and imagine the epic battles and adventures that took place on the screen.

Overall, there are so many reasons to visit New Zealand. From the adventure and natural beauty, to the unique culture and traditions, there is truly something for everyone in New Zealand.

Welcome to our travel guide to New Zealand! Nestled in the southwestern Pacific Ocean, New Zealand is a land of breathtaking natural beauty, rich culture, and endless adventure. From the bustling cities of Auckland and Wellington to the tranquil countryside and stunning national parks, New Zealand has something for everyone. In this guide, we will take you on a journey through the best of what New Zealand has to offer, from its vibrant cities and beautiful landscapes to its rich culture and delicious food and drink. So come along and explore the magic of New Zealand with us!

Robyn Russel

Chapter 1: General information about New Zealand

New Zealand is a country located in the southwestern Pacific Ocean. It consists of two main islands, the North and South Islands, as well as several smaller islands. New Zealand is known for its stunning natural beauty, with snow-capped mountains, lush forests, beautiful beaches, and crystal-clear lakes. It is also home to a unique and diverse range of flora and fauna, including many species that are found nowhere else in the world.

The capital of New Zealand is Wellington, located on the southern tip of the North Island. The largest city is Auckland, located on the northeastern coast of the North Island. English and Maori are New Zealand's two official languages. The country has a population of around 5 million people.

New Zealand has a parliamentary democracy and a constitutional monarchy, with Queen Elizabeth II as the head of state. The government is made up of a Parliament, which consists of the House of Representatives and the Senate. New Zealand is a member of the United Nations, the World Trade Organization, and the Commonwealth of Nations, among other international organizations.

The economy of New Zealand is largely based on agriculture, tourism, and trade. The country is known for its high-quality agricultural products, including dairy, meat, and wool. It is also a popular destination for tourists, who come to experience the country's stunning natural beauty and unique culture.

Interesting facts and figures

- New Zealand was the first country in the world to give women the right to vote, in 1893.
- The official languages of New Zealand are English and Maori, but many people also speak other languages, such as Samoan, Hindi, and Chinese.
- New Zealand is home to the kiwi, a flightless bird that is the national symbol of the country.

- The national rugby team of New Zealand, the All Blacks, is one of the most successful and famous sports teams in the world.
- The Maori name for New Zealand is "Aotearoa," which means "land of the long white cloud."
- New Zealand is home to the world's longest place name, "Taumatawhakatangihangakoauauotamateaturipukakapikimaungahoronukupokaiwenuakitanatahu," which is a hill in the Hawke's Bay region.
- The Lord of the Rings film, based on the books by J.R.R. Tolkien, was filmed entirely in New Zealand.
- New Zealand is home to many unique species of flora and fauna, including the tuatara, a reptile that is the only survivor of an ancient group of reptiles called the Sphenodontia.
- New Zealand is a popular destination for adventure sports, such as bungee jumping, skydiving, and rafting.

The geography and climate of New Zealand

New Zealand is located in the southwestern Pacific Ocean, east of Australia. The country is made up of two main islands, the North Island and the South Island, as well as several smaller islands. The North Island is the more populous of the two main islands, with a population of around 3.8 million people, while the South Island has a population of around 1.1 million people.

The North Island is mostly made up of low-lying hills and plains, with several active and inactive volcanoes. The South Island is more mountainous, with the Southern Alps running the length of the island. The highest peak in New Zealand is Mount Cook, which stands at an elevation of 3,724 meters (12,218 feet).

New Zealand has a temperate maritime climate, with mild temperatures, plenty of rainfall, and high levels of humidity. The average temperature in New Zealand varies depending on the region but generally ranges from 10 to 20 degrees Celsius (50 to 68 degrees Fahrenheit). The

North Island is generally warmer than the South Island, with temperatures ranging from 10 to 25 degrees Celsius (50 to 77 degrees Fahrenheit). The South Island is cooler, with temperatures ranging from 5 to 20 degrees Celsius (41 to 68 degrees Fahrenheit).

New Zealand is known for its high levels of rainfall, especially in the west of the country. The wettest months are usually June to August, while the driest months are December to February. However, the weather in New Zealand can be unpredictable, and it is not uncommon for all four seasons to be experienced in one day.

Robyn Russel

Chapter 2: Planning your trip to New Zealand

If you're planning a trip to New Zealand, there are a few things you should know to make your trip as smooth and enjoyable as possible.

First, you will need to arrange for a visa to enter New Zealand. Most visitors to New Zealand can apply for a visitor visa online, which allows them to stay in the country for up to nine months. However, if you plan to stay in New Zealand for longer than nine months, or if you plan to work or study while you're there, you will need to apply for a different type of visa.

Next, you will need to plan where to stay in New Zealand. There are many different types of accommodation available, from hotels and motels to hostels and campsites. You can also rent a holiday home or apartment, or stay with a local family through a homestay program.

When it comes to packing for your trip to New Zealand, you will need to bring warm and waterproof clothing, as the weather can be unpredictable. You should also bring comfortable walking shoes, as there are many beautiful hiking trails and outdoor activities in New Zealand. It's also a good idea to bring sunscreen, a hat, and insect repellent, as the sun can be strong in New Zealand, and there are some insects that can be pesky.

Finally, it's a good idea to plan out your itinerary in advance, to make the most of your time in New Zealand. There are many things to see and do in the country, from exploring the vibrant cities and beautiful landscapes to experiencing the unique culture and traditions of the Maori people. With careful planning, you can create the perfect trip to New Zealand!

How to get there

There are several ways to get to New Zealand, depending on where you are coming from. The most common way to get to New Zealand is by plane. There are several international airports in New Zealand, including Auckland Airport, Wellington Airport, and Christchurch Airport. Many major airlines offer flights to New Zealand, including Air New Zealand, Qantas, and Singapore Airlines. The flight from Los Angeles to Auckland, for example, takes around 12 hours.

Another way to get to New Zealand is by cruise ship. There are several cruise lines that offer itineraries that include stops in New Zealand, such as Princess Cruises and Celebrity Cruises. These cruises typically depart from Australia or the South Pacific and can take several weeks to complete.

It is also possible to get to New Zealand by ferry from Australia. The ferry from Sydney to Wellington, for example, takes around three days. This option is not as common, but it can be a great way to see both Australia and New Zealand on one trip.

Visa requirements

Most visitors to New Zealand will need to apply for a visa before they can enter the country. The type of visa you need will depend on the purpose of your trip, and how long you plan to stay in New Zealand.

The most common type of visa for visitors to New Zealand is the visitor visa. This visa allows you to stay in New Zealand for up to nine months and can be used for tourism, visiting family and friends, or short-term study. To apply for a visitor visa, you will need to fill out an online application, and provide some supporting documents, such as a passport, proof of funds, and evidence of your travel plans.

If you plan to stay in New Zealand for longer than nine months, or if you want to work or study while you're there, you will need to apply for a different type of visa. Some examples of other types of visas for New Zealand include the working holiday visa, the student visa, and the resident visa. To apply for these visas, you will need to provide additional documentation, such as proof of employment or enrollment in a school or university.

It's important to note that visa requirements for New Zealand can change over time, so it's always best to check with the New Zealand immigration website for the most up-to-date information.

Where to stay

There are many different types of accommodation available in New Zealand, to suit a variety of budgets and preferences. Some of the most common types of accommodation in New Zealand include hotels and motels, hostels, campsites, holiday homes and apartments, and homestays.

Hotels and motels are the most traditional type of accommodation in New Zealand. They offer a range of room types, from single rooms to family suites, and typically include amenities such as private bathrooms, televisions, and internet access. Hotels and motels can be found in most cities and towns in New Zealand, and are often the most convenient option for travelers.

Hostels are another popular option for accommodation in New Zealand. Hostels are typically more affordable than hotels and motels and offer shared dormitory-style rooms, as well as private rooms. Hostels are a great option for budget-conscious travelers and often have a social atmosphere, with common areas and activities.

Campsites are another option for travelers who want to experience the great outdoors of New Zealand. There are many campsites throughout the country, ranging from basic facilities to full-service campsites with showers, electricity, and other amenities. Camping is a popular way to explore New Zealand, and many campsites are located near popular hiking and outdoor activities.

Holiday homes and apartments are other options for travelers who want a more private and self-contained experience. These types of accommodations are typically rented out by the night or week, and come fully furnished with a kitchen, living room, and private bedrooms.

Holiday homes and apartments can be a great option for families or groups of friends traveling together.

Homestays are another unique way to experience New Zealand. A homestay involves staying with a local family in their home and can be a great way to learn about the culture and customs of New Zealand. Homestays typically include meals and other services and are a great option for travelers who want a more immersive and personal experience.

What to pack

When packing for your trip to New Zealand, it's important to consider the unpredictable weather and the many outdoor activities that are available in the country. Here are some things to consider packing for your trip to New Zealand:

Warm and waterproof clothing: The weather in New Zealand can be unpredictable, with all four seasons sometimes experienced in one day. It's a good idea to pack clothes that can be layered, as well as a waterproof jacket and pants.

Comfortable walking shoes: New Zealand is a great destination for hiking and outdoor activities, so it's important to pack comfortable shoes that are suitable for walking on a variety of terrain.

Sunscreen, a hat, and insect repellent: The sun can be strong in New Zealand, especially in the summer months, so it's important to protect yourself with sunscreen and a hat. Insect repellent can also be useful, as there are some insects in New Zealand that can be pesky.

Travel documents and important items: Make sure to pack your passport and any other important travel documents, as well as any medications or other items that you may need during your trip.

Camera and other electronics: New Zealand is full of beautiful landscapes and unique experiences, so it's a good idea to bring a camera or other electronic devices to capture your memories. Make sure to pack any necessary chargers and adapters.

Overall, the key to packing for a trip to New Zealand is to be prepared for a range of weather conditions and to bring comfortable and practical clothing and gear for outdoor activities.

Robyn Russel

Chapter 3: The North Island: Cities, culture, and adventure

The major cities of the North Island

The North Island of New Zealand is home to many of the country's major cities, each with its own unique character and attractions. Here are some of the major cities of the North Island:

Auckland: Auckland is the largest city in New Zealand, and is known for its vibrant culture, beautiful landscapes, and diverse population. Some of the top attractions in Auckland include the Sky Tower, the Auckland Museum, and the Waitakere Ranges.

Wellington: Wellington is the capital city of New Zealand, and is known for its cultural scene, café culture, and stunning harbor. Some of the top attractions in Wellington include the Te Papa Museum, the Wellington Cable Car, and the Weta Workshop.

Hamilton: Hamilton is the fourth-largest city in New Zealand, and is located in the Waikato region. It is known for its beautiful gardens, and the Hamilton Gardens are a popular attraction. Other attractions in Hamilton include the Waikato Museum, the Hamilton Zoo, and the Mighty River Domain.

Tauranga: Tauranga is a city on the Bay of Plenty, and is known for its beautiful beaches and outdoor activities. Some of the top attractions in Tauranga include Mount Maunganui Beach, the Tauranga Art Gallery, and the Tauranga Botanical Gardens.

Napier: Napier is a city on the east coast of the North Island, and is known for its Art

Cultural attractions and events

New Zealand is a country with a rich and diverse culture, and there are many cultural attractions and events to explore during your trip. Some examples of cultural attractions and events in New Zealand include:

Maori cultural experiences: The Maori are the indigenous people of New Zealand, and their culture is an important part of the country's heritage. Many Maori cultural experiences are available in New Zealand, such as guided tours of Maori villages, performances of traditional Maori dance and music, and workshops on Maori crafts and activities.

Museums and art galleries: New Zealand has many museums and art galleries that showcase the country's history, culture, and art. Some examples include the Te Papa Museum in Wellington, the Auckland Museum, and the Christchurch Art Gallery.

Music and performing arts: New Zealand is home to a vibrant music and performing arts scene, and there are many concerts, performances, and festivals throughout the year. Some examples include the New Zealand Symphony Orchestra, the New Zealand International Arts Festival, and the Auckland Arts Festival.

Food and drink: New Zealand is known for its delicious food and drink, and there are many opportunities to try local specialties, such as lamb, seafood, and kiwifruit. There are also many wineries and breweries in New Zealand, offering tastings and tours of their facilities.

Overall, there are many cultural attractions and events in New Zealand, and taking the time to explore these can give you a deeper understanding and appreciation of the country's unique culture and heritage.

Chapter 4: The South Island: Natural beauty and outdoor activities

The major cities of the South Island

The South Island of New Zealand is home to many of the country's major cities, each with its own unique character and attractions. Here are some of the major cities of the South Island:

Christchurch: Christchurch is the largest city on the South Island, and is known for its gardens, parks, and cultural attractions. Some of the top attractions in Christchurch include the Christchurch Botanic Gardens, the Canterbury Museum, and the International Antarctic Centre.

Dunedin: Dunedin is a city on the east coast of the South Island, and is known for its Scottish heritage, wildlife, and universities. Some of the top attractions in Dunedin include the Otago Peninsula, the Dunedin Railway Station, and the University of Otago.

Queenstown: Queenstown is a popular tourist destination on the shores of Lake Wakatipu, and is known for its adventure sports and beautiful scenery. Some of the top attractions in Queenstown include the Skyline Gondola, the Shotover Jet, and the Kawarau Bridge Bungy.

Nelson: Nelson is a city on the north coast of the South Island, and is known for its art and craft scene, beautiful beaches, and national parks. Some of the top attractions in Nelson include the Abel Tasman National Park, the World of WearableArt and Classic Cars Museum, and the Nelson Market.

Invercargill: Invercargill is the southernmost city in New Zealand, and is known for its historical buildings and wildlife. Some of the top attractions in Invercargill include the Southland Museum and Art Gallery, the Queen's Park, and the Invercargill Brewery.

Overall, the South Island of New Zealand offers a diverse range of experiences, from bustling cities and cultural attractions, to stunning landscapes and outdoor adventure.

Whether you're a city-slicker or a nature lover, there's something for everyone on the South Island.

Natural attractions and national parks

New Zealand is known for its stunning natural beauty, and there are many natural attractions and national parks to explore during your trip. Some examples of natural attractions and national parks in New Zealand include:

Fiordland National Park: Fiordland National Park is a World Heritage site on the southwest coast of the South Island, known for its beautiful fiords, waterfalls, and forests. Some popular attractions in Fiordland National Park include the Milford Track, the Doubtful Sound, and the Kepler Track.

Abel Tasman National Park: Abel Tasman National Park is a coastal national park on the north coast of the South Island, known for its beautiful beaches, forests, and wildlife. Some popular attractions in Abel Tasman National Park include the Abel Tasman Coast Track, the Kayak Abel Tasman, and the Abel Tasman Sea Shuttle.

Tongariro National Park: Tongariro National Park is a World Heritage site on the central plateau of the North Island, known for its volcanoes, lakes, and forests. Some popular attractions in Tongariro National Park include the Tongariro Alpine Crossing, the Whakapapa Village, and the Tongariro Northern Circuit.

Aoraki/Mount Cook National Park: Aoraki/Mount Cook National Park is a national park on the South Island, known for its mountains, glaciers, and alpine lakes. Some popular attractions in Aoraki/Mount Cook National Park include the Aoraki/Mount Cook Village, the Tasman Glacier, and the Hooker Valley Track.

Paparoa National Park: Paparoa National Park is a national park on the west coast of the South Island, known for its limestone caves and karst landscapes. Some popular attractions in Paparoa National Park include the Punakaiki Pancake Rocks and Blowholes, the Cave Stream Scenic Reserve, and the Paparoa Track.

Overall, New Zealand is home to many beautiful natural attractions and national parks, and exploring these can be a highlight of your trip to New Zealand. Whether you want to hike through beautiful forests, admire stunning lakes and mountains, or explore underground caves, there are many opportunities to experience the natural beauty of New Zealand.

Outdoor activities and adventure sports

New Zealand is a paradise for outdoor enthusiasts, with its stunning landscapes and wide range of outdoor activities and adventure sports. Some examples of outdoor activities and adventure sports in New Zealand include:

Hiking and tramping: New Zealand has many beautiful hiking and tramping trails, ranging from easy walks to multi-day expeditions. Some popular hiking destinations in New Zealand include the Tongariro Alpine Crossing, the Abel Tasman Coast Track, and the Kepler Track.

Skiing and snowboarding: New Zealand is home to several ski fields, offering skiing and snowboarding opportunities in the winter months. Some popular ski fields in New Zealand include Whakapapa and Turoa on

Mount Ruapehu, Coronet Peak, and The Remarkables near Queenstown.

Water sports: New Zealand has many beautiful beaches and lakes, offering opportunities for water sports such as surfing, kayaking, and sailing. Some popular water sports destinations in New Zealand include the Bay of Islands, the Abel Tasman National Park, and Lake Wanaka.

Bungee jumping: New Zealand is known for its bungee jumping, and there are several bungee jumping sites throughout the country. Some popular bungee jumping sites in New Zealand include the Kawarau Bridge near Queenstown, the Nevis Bungy near Wanaka, and the Taupo Bungy.

Overall, New Zealand offers a wide range of outdoor activities and adventure sports and is a great destination for travelers who love the great outdoors. Whether you're a seasoned adventurer or a beginner, there are many opportunities to explore and enjoy the natural beauty of New Zealand.

Robyn Russel

Chapter 5: Maori culture and traditions

The history and culture of the Maori people

The Maori are the indigenous people of New Zealand, and their history and culture are an important part of the country's heritage. The Maori are Polynesian and are believed to have arrived in New Zealand around 1300 AD. They developed a unique culture, with a strong emphasis on family, community, and spirituality.

Maori culture is based on a set of traditions and customs known as Tikanga Maori. These traditions include the Maori language, known as Te Reo, as well as art, dance, and music. Maori art is known for its intricate carving and weaving and is often based on natural themes, such as plants and animals. Maori dance, known as haka, is a powerful and expressive form of dance that is often performed at events and ceremonies.

The Maori have a strong spiritual connection to the land and believe that their ancestors continue to reside in the natural world. This connection is expressed through traditional practices such as the karakia, a form of prayer, and the powhiri, a traditional Maori welcome ceremony.

Today, the Maori are an important part of New Zealand society, and their culture is celebrated and preserved through events, festivals, and cultural experiences. Many Maori cultural experiences are available in New Zealand, such as guided tours of Maori villages, performances of traditional Maori dance and music, and workshops on Maori crafts and activities.

Overall, the history and culture of the Maori people are an essential part of the identity of New Zealand, and learning about and experiencing Maori culture can be a highlight of your trip to the country.

Traditional Maori arts and crafts

The Maori are known for their rich and diverse artistic traditions, and their art and crafts are an important part of their culture. Some examples of traditional Maori arts and crafts include:

Carving: Maori carving is known for its intricate and detailed designs, which often depict natural themes such as plants and animals. Traditional Maori carvings are made from materials such as wood, bone, and stone, and are used to decorate objects such as buildings, canoes, and weapons.

Weaving: Maori weaving is an ancient art form, and is used to create a wide range of items, including baskets, mats, and clothing. Traditional Maori weaving techniques use materials such as flax, harakeke, and kiekie, and the patterns and designs often have cultural and spiritual significance.

Tattooing: Maori tattooing, known as ta moko, is an important part of Maori culture, and is used to express an individual's identity, heritage, and status. Traditional Maori tattoos are created using chisels and a mallet and are often applied to the face, thighs, and buttocks.

Painting: Maori painting is an important part of Maori art, and is used to create a wide range of items, including carvings, clothing, and tattoos. Traditional Maori painting techniques use natural materials such as earth pigments and plant dyes, and the patterns and designs often have cultural and spiritual significance.

Overall, traditional Maori arts and crafts are a fascinating and unique aspect of Maori culture, and learning about and experiencing these can be a highlight of your trip to New Zealand.

Maori cultural experiences and performances

Many Maori cultural experiences and performances are available in New Zealand, offering visitors the opportunity to learn about and experience Maori culture firsthand. Some examples of Maori cultural experiences and performances **include:**

Guided tours of Maori villages: Many Maori cultural centers and museums offer guided tours of traditional Maori villages, where visitors can learn about the history, culture, and customs of the Maori people. These tours often include demonstrations of traditional Maori activities, such as carving, weaving, and fishing.

Performances of traditional Maori dance and music: Traditional Maori dance and music are an important part of Maori culture, and many Maori cultural centers and museums offer performances of these art forms. The haka is a particularly well-known form of Maori dance and is a powerful and expressive performance often seen at events and ceremonies.

Workshops on Maori crafts and activities: Many Maori cultural centers and museums offer workshops on traditional Maori crafts and activities, such as carving, weaving, and tattooing. These workshops provide an opportunity to learn about and try these activities for yourself and often include demonstrations and guidance from experienced practitioners.

Maori cultural feasts and events: Many Maori cultural centers and museums offer feasts and events that showcase Maori culture and traditions. These may include traditional Maori food and drink, performances of dance and music, and other activities and experiences.

Overall, experiencing Maori cultural experiences and performances can be a highlight of your trip to New Zealand, and can provide an in-depth look at the rich and diverse culture of the Maori people.

Chapter 6: The best food and drink in New Zealand

New Zealand is known for its delicious food and drink, and there are many opportunities to try local specialties during your trip. Some examples of the best food and drink in New Zealand include:

Lamb: New Zealand lamb is renowned for its flavor and quality, and is a popular ingredient in many dishes. Some popular dishes featuring lamb include roast lamb with mint sauce, lamb kebabs, and lamb curry.

Seafood: New Zealand has a long coastline, and is known for its delicious seafood, including fish, shellfish, and crayfish. Some popular dishes featuring seafood include fish and chips, mussels in white wine sauce, and paua (abalone) fritters.

Kiwifruit: The kiwifruit is native to New Zealand, and is a popular and nutritious fruit. Kiwifruit can be eaten fresh or used in a variety of dishes, such as kiwifruit salad, kiwifruit smoothies, and kiwifruit sorbet.

Wine: New Zealand is home to many wineries, that produce a wide range of high-quality wines. Some popular wines from New Zealand include Sauvignon Blanc from Marlborough, Pinot Noir from Central Otago, and Riesling from the Gisborne region.

Beer: New Zealand is also home to many breweries, producing a range of tasty craft beers. Some popular beers from New Zealand include Monteith's, Tui, and Speight's.

In addition to the food and drink mentioned above, there are many other delicious options to try in New Zealand. Some other examples of the best food and drink in New Zealand include:

Pavlova: Pavlova is a popular dessert in New Zealand, and is made from a meringue base topped with whipped cream and fruit. The pavlova is believed to have been created in New Zealand or Australia and is named after the Russian ballerina Anna Pavlova.

Fush and Chups: Fush and chups (pronounced "foosh and choops") is a popular snack in New Zealand, consisting of battered and fried fish and chips. This dish is a favorite at beachside fish and chip shops and is often served with lemon, tartare sauce, and vinegar.

Hangi: The hangi is a traditional Maori cooking method, where food is cooked in an underground oven. The hangi is often used for special occasions, and the food is typically placed in a pit lined with hot rocks and covered with earth to cook.

Lamingtons: Lamingtons are a popular dessert in New Zealand, and are made from squares of sponge cake coated in chocolate icing and desiccated coconut. The lamington is believed to have been named after Lord Lamington, the Governor of Queensland in Australia.

Kumera: Kumera (also known as sweet potato) is a popular ingredient in New Zealand cuisine, and is often used in dishes such as kumera pie, kumera chips, and kumera and apple rosti. Kumera is a traditional Maori crop and was an important food source for Maori communities. Kumera is now a popular ingredient in modern New Zealand cuisine and is enjoyed for its sweet and starchy flavor.

New Zealand has a vibrant food and drink scene and trying local specialties can be a highlight of your trip to the country. Whether you're a foodie or just looking for a tasty meal, there are many delicious options to explore in New Zealand.

Traditional Maori cuisine

Traditional Maori cuisine is an important part of Maori culture and has been influenced by both the local environment and Polynesian traditions. Some examples of traditional Maori cuisine include:

Hangi: The hangi is a traditional Maori cooking method, where food is cooked in an underground oven. The hangi is often used for special occasions, and the food is typically placed in a pit lined with hot rocks and covered with earth to cook.

Kumera: Kumera (also known as sweet potato) is a traditional Maori crop, and was an important food source for Maori communities. Kumera is often cooked in the hangi and is enjoyed for its sweet and starchy flavor.

Eel: Eel is a traditional Maori food, and is often caught and cooked in the hangi. Eel is a tasty and nutritious food, and is enjoyed for its tender and succulent flesh.

Paua: Paua (abalone) is a traditional Maori food, and is often harvested from the rocky coastlines of New Zealand. Paua is a delicacy and is often eaten raw, or cooked in the hangi or on a barbecue.

Watercress: Watercress is a traditional Maori food, and is often gathered from rivers and streams. Watercress is a tasty and nutritious green and is often eaten raw or cooked in the hangi.

Hāngī pīwariwari: Hāngī pīwariwari is a traditional Maori dish made from breadfruit, which is steamed in the hangi. Breadfruit is a starchy and nutritious fruit and is often used as a substitute for potatoes in Maori cuisine.

Kāretu: Kāretu is a traditional Maori dish made from kāretu berries, which are native to New Zealand. Kāretu berries are small and sweet and are often used to make jams and jellies.

Kūmara: Kūmara (also known as sweet potato) is a traditional Maori crop, and was an important food source for Maori communities. Kūmara is often cooked in the hangi and is enjoyed for its sweet and starchy flavor.

Tītī: Tītī (muttonbird) is a traditional Maori food, and is often harvested from the nests of the sooty shearwater bird. Tītī is a delicacy and is often cooked in the hangi or on a barbecue.

Whaiaroaro: Whaiaroaro is a traditional Maori dish made from fernroot, which is steamed in the hangi. Fernroot is a starchy and nutritious vegetable and is often used as a substitute for potatoes in Maori cuisine.

Overall, traditional Maori cuisine is an important and delicious part of Maori culture and trying these dishes can be a highlight of your trip to New Zealand. Many Maori cultural centers and museums offer traditional Maori feasts, where you can try a variety of dishes and learn about their cultural significance.

Regional specialties and local delicacies

In addition to the food and drink mentioned above, there are many regional specialties and local delicacies to try in New Zealand. Some examples of these regional specialties and local delicacies include:

Whitebait fritters: Whitebait fritters are a popular dish in New Zealand, and are made from whitebait, which is small juvenile fish. Whitebait fritters are often served with lemon and tartare sauce and are a favorite at beachside fish and chip shops.

Pāua fritters: Pāua fritters are a popular dish in New Zealand, and are made from pāua (abalone), which is a delicacy in Maori cuisine. Pāua fritters are often served with lemon and tartare sauce and are a favorite at beachside fish and chip shops.

Fish pie: Fish pie is a popular dish in New Zealand, and is made from a mixture of fish, potatoes, and other vegetables, topped with a creamy sauce and a pastry crust. Fish pie is a comfort food, and is often enjoyed on cold and rainy days.

Kōura: Kōura (crayfish) is a popular delicacy in New Zealand, and is often caught and cooked in the country's many rivers and lakes. Kōura is a tasty and succulent seafood and is often served with butter and lemon.

Pavlova: Pavlova is a popular dessert in New Zealand, and is made from a meringue base topped with whipped cream and fruit. The pavlova is believed to have been created in New Zealand or Australia and is named after the Russian ballerina Anna Pavlova.

New Zealand has many regional specialties and local delicacies to try, and exploring these can be a highlight of your trip to the country. Whether you're a foodie or just looking for something tasty to eat, there are many delicious options to explore in New Zealand.

The best places to eat and drink in New Zealand

New Zealand is home to many great places to eat and drink, and there are many opportunities to try local specialties and regional delicacies during your trip. Some examples of New Zealand's best places to eat and drink include:

Beachside fish and chip shops: Many of New Zealand's beaches and coastal towns have traditional fish and chip shops, where you can try delicious seafood, such as fish, pāua (abalone), and kōura (crayfish). These shops are often popular spots for locals and tourists alike and offer a relaxed and informal atmosphere.

Farmers' markets: Many of New Zealand's cities and towns have farmers' markets, where you can buy fresh and local produce, as well as prepared foods, such as pies, sandwiches, and cakes. These markets are a great way to try delicious and seasonal foods and support local farmers and producers.

Wineries: New Zealand is home to many wineries that produce a wide range of high-quality wines. Many of these wineries offer tastings and tours, and some also have restaurants or cafes where you can try local wines and dishes.

Breweries: New Zealand is also home to many breweries, producing a range of tasty craft beers. Many of these breweries offer tastings and tours, and some also have taprooms or pubs where you can try their beers and other **drinks.**

Maori cultural centers and museums: Many Maori cultural centers and museums offer traditional Maori feasts, where you can try a variety of dishes and learn about their cultural significance. These feasts are a great way to experience Maori cuisine and culture and are often accompanied by performances of traditional Maori dance and music.

In addition to the places to eat and drink mentioned above, there are many other great options to explore in New Zealand. Some examples of other places to eat and drink in New Zealand include:

Cafes: New Zealand is home to many great cafes, offering a wide range of delicious and affordable food and drink. These cafes often serve breakfast, lunch, and snacks, and are popular spots for locals and tourists alike.

Pubs and bars: New Zealand has a vibrant pub and bar scene, and many of these establishments offer tasty food, local beers and wines, and a friendly atmosphere. Some pubs and bars also have live music or sports events, making them a great place to relax and unwind.

Fine dining restaurants: New Zealand is home to many fine dining restaurants, offering high-quality food, service, and atmosphere. These restaurants often serve local and seasonal ingredients, and may also have a focus on a particular cuisine or style of cooking.

Street food vendors: Many of New Zealand's cities and towns have street food vendors, offering a wide range of tasty and affordable food. These vendors may serve dishes such as burgers, hot dogs, falafel, and dumplings, and are a great option for a quick and tasty meal.

Overall, there are many great places to eat and drink in New Zealand, and exploring these can be a highlight of your trip to the country. Whether you're looking for fine dining, casual eats, or something in between, there are many options to choose from in New Zealand.

Chapter 7: The most iconic film locations in New Zealand

New Zealand is a popular destination for filmmakers and has been the location for many iconic and memorable films. Some examples of the most iconic film locations in New Zealand include:

The Lord of the Rings film trilogy: As mentioned above, the Lord of the Rings film trilogy was shot in New Zealand, and many of the film's locations, such as Hobbiton and Mount Sunday, have become popular tourist attractions.

The Hobbit film trilogy: The Hobbit film trilogy, a prequel to the Lord of the Rings trilogy, was also shot in New Zealand, and many of the film's locations, such as the Shire and Rivendell, can be visited during your trip to the country.

The Chronicles of Narnia: The Lion, the Witch, and the Wardrobe: The Chronicles of Narnia: The Lion, the Witch, and the Wardrobe was shot in New Zealand, and many of the film's locations, such as the Beech Forest and Mount Aspiring National Park, can be visited during your trip to the country.

King Kong: King Kong was shot in New Zealand, and many of the film's locations, such as Skull Island and the city of New York, were created using miniature sets and special effects.

The Piano: The Piano was shot in New Zealand, and many of the film's locations, such as the West Coast and Fiordland National Park, are beautiful and scenic.

In addition to the iconic film locations mentioned above, there are many other memorable and scenic places to visit in New Zealand. Some examples of other iconic film locations in New Zealand include:

The Last Samurai: The Last Samurai was shot in New Zealand, and many of the film's locations, such as Himeji Castle and Mount Taranaki, are beautiful and historic.

Whale Rider: Whale Rider was shot in New Zealand, and many of the film's locations, such as Whangara and the East Cape, are scenic and culturally significant.

The Water Horse: Legend of the Deep: The Water Horse: Legend of the Deep was shot in New Zealand, and many of the film's locations, such as Loch Ness and Glenorchy, are scenic and beautiful.

The Lion, the Witch, and the Wardrobe: The Lion, the Witch, and the Wardrobe was shot in New Zealand, and many of the film's locations, such as the forest of Aslan and the glacier of Jadis, are beautiful and magical.

The Avengers: Age of Ultron: The Avengers: Age of Ultron was shot in New Zealand, and many of the film's locations, such as the city of Sokovia and the forest of Hawkeye, are stunning and memorable.

There are many iconic and memorable film locations to visit in New Zealand, and exploring these can be a highlight of your trip to the country. Whether you're a fan of these films or just looking for beautiful and scenic places to visit, there are many options to choose from in New Zealand.

How to visit the film locations and experience the magic for yourself

Visiting film locations in New Zealand can be a great way to experience the magic of the films and the beauty of the country. Some tips for visiting film locations in New Zealand include:

Research the locations: Before you visit, do some research to find out where the film locations are, and what you can expect to see and do there. This will help you plan your trip and use your time wisely.

Use a map: Many of the film locations in New Zealand are spread out across the country, so it can be helpful to use a map to plan your route and find the best way to get there. You can also use a map to find nearby attractions, accommodations, and other facilities.

Take a tour: Many of the film locations in New Zealand offer guided tours, which can be a great way to learn more about the films and the locations. These tours are often led by knowledgeable and experienced guides, who can provide insight and information about the films and the locations.

Be prepared: Some of the film locations in New Zealand are in remote or rugged areas, so it's important to be prepared for the weather and the terrain. This may include packing appropriate clothing, footwear, and supplies, and being aware of any safety considerations.

Take photos: Many of the film locations in New Zealand are beautiful and memorable, so be sure to take plenty of photos to capture the experience. You can also use these photos to share your trip with friends and family and to remember the magic of the films and the beauty of New Zealand.

Overall, visiting film locations in New Zealand can be a great way to experience the magic of the films and the beauty of the country. With some research, planning, and preparation, you can visit these locations and experience the magic for yourself.

The Lord of the Rings film locations in New Zealand

New Zealand is the home of the Lord of the Rings film trilogy, and many of the film's locations can be visited during your trip to the country. Some examples of Lord of the Rings film locations in New Zealand include:

Hobbiton: Hobbiton is a village built for the Lord of the Rings films, and is located in Matamata, in the Waikato region of the North Island. Hobbiton is now a popular tourist attraction, and visitors can take guided tours of the village, including the Hobbit holes, the Mill, and the Green Dragon Inn.

Mount Victoria: Mount Victoria is a mountain located in Wellington, on the North Island of New Zealand. Mount Victoria was used as a filming location for the Lord of the Rings films and is featured in the opening scenes of The Fellowship of the Ring.

Mount Ngauruhoe: Mount Ngauruhoe is a volcano located in the Tongariro National Park, on the North Island of New Zealand. Mount Ngauruhoe was used as a filming location for the Lord of the Rings films and is depicted as Mount Doom in the films.

Mount Sunday: Mount Sunday is a mountain located in the Canterbury region of the South Island of New Zealand. Mount Sunday was used as a filming location for the Lord of the Rings films and is depicted as Edoras, the capital of Rohan, in the films.

Paradise: Paradise is a small town located near Glenorchy, in the Otago region of the South Island of New Zealand. Paradise was used as a filming location for the Lord of the Rings films and is featured in many scenes, including the journey to Isengard, the Argonath, and the Battle of Amon Hen.

Visiting Lord of the Rings film locations in New Zealand can be a highlight of your trip to the country, and is a must for fans of the films. Many of these locations are beautiful and scenic and offer a glimpse into the world of Middle-earth.

The history of the Lord of the Rings films in New Zealand

The Lord of the Rings film trilogy was produced and filmed in New Zealand and has played an important role in the country's culture and history. The films were directed by Peter Jackson, a New Zealand filmmaker, and were based on the novels by J.R.R. Tolkien.

The first Lord of the Rings film, The Fellowship of the Ring, was released in 2001 and was followed by The Two Towers in 2002, and The Return of the King in 2003. The films were shot back-to-back and featured a large and talented cast and crew, many of whom were from New Zealand.

The Lord of the Rings films were a huge success, both commercially and critically, and helped to put New Zealand on the map as a filmmaking destination. The films won 17 Academy Awards, including Best Picture for The

Return of the King, and were a major boost to the New Zealand film industry.

In addition to their impact on the film industry, the Lord of the Rings films also had a significant cultural impact in New Zealand. Many of the film's locations, such as Hobbiton, Mount Victoria, and Mount Ngauruhoe, have become popular tourist attractions, and the films have helped to promote New Zealand as a unique and beautiful destination.

The history of the Lord of the Rings films in New Zealand is an important and fascinating part of the country's culture and history. The films have had a lasting impact on the country, and continue to be a source of pride and inspiration for many New Zealanders.

In addition to the Lord of the Rings film locations mentioned above, there are many other places in New Zealand that were used as filming locations for the trilogy. Some examples of other Lord of the Rings film locations in New Zealand include:

The Putangirua Pinnacles: The Putangirua Pinnacles are a series of unusual rock formations located near Palliser Bay, on the North Island of New Zealand. The Putangirua Pinnacles were used as a filming location for the Lord of the Rings films, and are depicted as the Paths of the Dead in the films.

The Pelennor Fields: The Pelennor Fields are a flat and open area located near Twizel, in the Canterbury region of the South Island of New Zealand. The Pelennor Fields were used as a filming location for the Lord of the Rings films, and are depicted as the battlefield where the Battle of the Pelennor Fields takes place in the films.

The Kaitoke Regional Park: The Kaitoke Regional Park is a scenic park located near Upper Hutt, on the North Island of New Zealand. The Kaitoke Regional Park was used as a filming location for the Lord of the Rings films and is depicted as the Elven forest of Rivendell in the films.

The River Anduin: The River Anduin is a river located in the Wakatipu Basin, in the Otago region of the South

Island of New Zealand. The River Anduin was used as a filming location for the Lord of the Rings films and is featured in many scenes, including the journey to Lothlórien and the Battle of the Pelennor Fields.

The Beech Forest: The Beech Forest is a scenic forest located near Te Anau, in the Fiordland region of the South Island of New Zealand. The Beech Forest was used as a filming location for the Lord of the Rings films and is depicted as the forest of Fangorn in the films.

Overall, there are many Lord of the Rings film locations to visit in New Zealand, and exploring these can be a highlight of your trip to the country. Whether you're a fan of films or just looking for beautiful and scenic places to visit, there are many options to choose from in New Zealand.

Robyn Russel

Chapter 8: Must-see landmarks and hidden gems

There are many other must-see landmarks and hidden gems to explore in New Zealand. Some examples of must-see landmarks and hidden gems in New Zealand include:

The Bay of Islands: The Bay of Islands is a scenic area located in the Northland region of the North Island of New Zealand. The Bay of Islands is known for its beautiful beaches, forests, and islands, and is a popular spot for activities such as boating, fishing, and swimming.

The Coromandel Peninsula: The Coromandel Peninsula is a scenic peninsula located on the North Island of New Zealand. The Coromandel Peninsula is known for its beautiful beaches, forests, and hot springs, and is a popular spot for activities such as hiking, camping, and swimming.

The Abel Tasman National Park: The Abel Tasman National Park is a scenic national park located on the

South Island of New Zealand. The Abel Tasman National Park is known for its beautiful beaches, forests, and mountains, and is a popular spot for activities such as hiking, kayaking, and swimming.

The Waitomo Caves: The Waitomo Caves are a series of underground caves located on the North Island of New Zealand. The Waitomo Caves are known for their stunning limestone formations and glowworms and are a popular spot for activities such as cave tubing, caving, and hiking.

The Milford Sound: The Milford Sound is a scenic fiord located in the Fiordland region of the South Island of New Zealand. The Milford Sound is known for its beautiful mountains, waterfalls, and wildlife, and is a popular spot for activities such as boating, hiking, and sightseeing.

The Sky Tower: The Sky Tower is a tall tower located in Auckland, on the North Island of New Zealand. The Sky Tower offers stunning views of the city and the surrounding area and is a popular spot for activities such as skywalking, sky jumping, and dining.

The Tongariro Alpine Crossing: The Tongariro Alpine Crossing is a popular hiking trail located in the Tongariro National Park, on the North Island of New Zealand. The Tongariro Alpine Crossing offers stunning views of the park and the surrounding area and is a popular spot for activities such as hiking, camping, and sightseeing.

The Catlins: The Catlins is a scenic area located on the South Island of New Zealand. The Catlins is known for its beautiful beaches, forests, and wildlife, and is a popular spot for activities such as hiking, camping, and surfing.

The Canterbury Plains: The Canterbury Plains is a flat and open area located on the South Island of New Zealand. The Canterbury Plains is known for its beautiful landscapes and is a popular spot for activities such as hiking, cycling, and sightseeing.

There are many must-see landmarks and hidden gems to explore in New Zealand, and discovering these can be a highlight of your trip to the country. Whether you're looking for beautiful scenery, outdoor adventure, or cultural experiences, there are many options to choose from in New Zealand.

The most popular landmarks and attractions in New Zealand

New Zealand is home to many popular landmarks and attractions, and these are some of the most visited and well-known destinations in the country:

The Sky Tower: The Sky Tower is a tall tower located in Auckland, on the North Island of New Zealand. The Sky Tower offers stunning views of the city and the surrounding area and is a popular spot for activities such as skywalking, skyjumping, and dining.

The Hobbiton Movie Set: The Hobbiton Movie Set is a film set located near Matamata, on the North Island of New Zealand. The Hobbiton Movie Set was used as a filming location for the Lord of the Rings and The Hobbit film trilogies and is a popular spot for fans of the films to visit.

The Milford Sound: The Milford Sound is a scenic fiord located in the Fiordland region of the South Island of New Zealand. The Milford Sound is known for its beautiful mountains, waterfalls, and wildlife, and is a popular spot for activities such as boating, hiking, and sightseeing.

The Rotorua Geothermal District: The Rotorua Geothermal District is a geothermal area located near Rotorua, on the North Island of New Zealand. The Rotorua Geothermal District is known for its hot springs, geysers, and mud pools, and is a popular spot for activities such as soaking, hiking, and sightseeing.

The Wai-O-Tapu Thermal Wonderland: The Wai-O-Tapu Thermal Wonderland is a geothermal area located near Rotorua, on the North Island of New Zealand. The Wai-O-Tapu Thermal Wonderland is known for its colorful hot springs, geysers, and mud pools, and is a popular spot for activities such as soaking, hiking, and sightseeing.

Overall, there are many popular landmarks and attractions to visit in New Zealand, and exploring these can be a highlight of your trip to the country. Whether you're looking for beautiful scenery, outdoor adventure, or cultural experiences, there are many options to choose from in New Zealand.

Secret spots and hidden gems off the beaten track

There are many other secret spots and hidden gems to explore in New Zealand. These are some examples of secret spots and hidden gems off the beaten track in New Zealand:

The Whanganui National Park: The Whanganui National Park is a scenic national park located on the North Island of New Zealand. The Whanganui National Park is known for its beautiful rivers, forests, and mountains, and is a popular spot for activities such as hiking, kayaking, and rafting.

The Kaimai-Mamaku Forest Park: The Kaimai-Mamaku Forest Park is a scenic forest park located on the North Island of New Zealand. The Kaimai-Mamaku Forest Park is known for its beautiful forests, waterfalls, and wildlife, and is a popular spot for activities such as hiking, camping, and birdwatching.

The Catlins: The Catlins is a scenic area located on the South Island of New Zealand. The Catlins is known for its beautiful beaches, forests, and wildlife, and is a popular spot for activities such as hiking, camping, and surfing.

The Stewart Island National Park: The Stewart Island National Park is a scenic national park located on Stewart Island, off the coast of the South Island of New Zealand. The Stewart Island National Park is known for its beautiful forests, beaches, and wildlife, and is a popular spot for activities such as hiking, birdwatching, and fishing.

The Abel Tasman Coast Track: The Abel Tasman Coast Track is a popular hiking trail located in the Abel Tasman National Park, on the South Island of New Zealand. The Abel Tasman Coast Track offers stunning views of the park and the surrounding area and is a popular spot for activities such as hiking, kayaking, and sightseeing.

Overall, there are many secret spots and hidden gems to explore in New Zealand, and discovering these can be a highlight of your trip to the country. Whether you're looking for beautiful scenery, outdoor adventure, or cultural experiences, there are many options to choose from in New Zealand.

Insider tips for experiencing the best of New Zealand

New Zealand is a beautiful and diverse country, and there are many ways to experience the best of what it has to offer. Here are some insider tips for experiencing the best of New Zealand:

Plan ahead: New Zealand is a popular destination, and many of the country's best attractions can be busy, especially during peak season. To avoid disappointment, it's a good idea to plan ahead and book tickets, tours, and accommodations in advance.

Get off the beaten track: While New Zealand has many popular landmarks and attractions, there are also many hidden gems and secret spots to explore. To experience the best of what the country has to offer, try to get off the beaten track and explore some of the less-visited areas.

Try something new: New Zealand is a great place to try new things, and there are many exciting activities and adventures to experience. Whether you're interested in outdoor sports, cultural experiences, or food and drink, there's something for everyone in New Zealand.

Be respectful: New Zealand has a rich and diverse culture, and it's important to be respectful when you visit. This includes respecting the local environment, the Maori culture, and the customs and traditions of the people who live there.

Have fun: Above all, the most important tip for experiencing the best of New Zealand is to have fun. New Zealand is a beautiful and exciting country, and there's so much to see and do. Enjoy your trip and make the most of your time in New Zealand.

In addition to the insider tips mentioned above, there are many other ways to experience the best of New Zealand. Here are some more tips for experiencing the best of what the country has to offer:

Visit during the shoulder season: New Zealand is a popular destination, and many of the country's attractions can be busy, especially during peak season. To avoid the crowds and get the best deals, try to visit during the shoulder season, which is typically in the spring or fall.

Rent a car: New Zealand is a large country, and many of the best attractions are located outside of the major cities. To explore these areas, it's a good idea to rent a car, which will give you the freedom and flexibility to visit the places you want to see.

Stay in a hostel: New Zealand is a popular destination, and accommodation can be expensive, especially in the major cities. To save money and meet other travelers, try staying in a hostel, which offers affordable and social accommodation.

Use a guidebook: New Zealand is a large and diverse country, and it can be overwhelming to plan your trip. To get the most out of your time in the country, consider using a guidebook, which can provide valuable information and tips for planning your trip.

Talk to the locals: New Zealanders are friendly and welcoming, and they can be a great source of information and advice. To learn more about the country and its culture, try to talk to the locals and ask for their recommendations and insights.

Overall, with some planning, flexibility, and local knowledge, you can experience the best of what New Zealand has to offer. Whether you're looking for beautiful scenery, outdoor adventure, or cultural experiences, there are many options to choose from in New Zealand.

Robyn Russel

Chapter 9: Tips for traveling like a local in New Zealand

To truly experience the best of what New Zealand has to offer, it's a good idea to try to travel like a local. Here are some tips for traveling like a local in New Zealand:

Learn some basic Maori phrases: New Zealand has a rich and diverse culture, and the Maori language is an important part of that culture. To show respect and appreciation for the Maori culture, try to learn some basic Maori phrases, such as "kia ora" (hello), "ka mau te wehi" (wow), and "noho ora mai" (take care).

Try the local food: New Zealand has a unique and delicious cuisine, and there are many local dishes and delicacies to try. To experience the best of what the country has to offer, try to sample some of the local food, such as hangi (food cooked in an earth oven), kiwifruit, and pavlova (a meringue-based dessert).

Shop at local markets: New Zealand has many local markets, which are great places to buy fresh produce, handmade crafts, and souvenirs. To support the local economy and get a true taste of the country, try to shop at local markets, such as the Otara Flea Market in Auckland or the Otago Farmers Market in Dunedin.

Stay in a homestay: New Zealand has many homestay options, which are a great way to experience the country like a local. Homestays are private homes that offer accommodation, and they can provide a unique and authentic experience of the country. To stay in a homestay, try to book through a local homestay agency or a platform such as Airbnb.

Join a tour or activity: New Zealand is a great place to try new things, and there are many local tours and activities to experience. To learn more about the country and its culture, try to join a tour or activity, such as a Maori cultural performance, a wine-tasting tour, or a hiking trip.

In addition to the tips mentioned above, there are many other ways to travel like a local in New Zealand. Here are some more tips for experiencing the country like a local:

Use public transport: New Zealand has a good public transport system, and it's a great way to get around the country like a local. To use public transport, try to buy a New Zealand Rail Pass, which will give you access to trains and buses throughout the country.

Stay in a bed and breakfast: New Zealand has many bed and breakfast options, which are a great way to experience the country like a local. Bed and breakfasts are private homes that offer accommodation and breakfast, and they can provide a unique and authentic experience of the country. To stay in a bed and breakfast, try to book through a local bed and breakfast agency or a platform such as Airbnb.

Visit a local festival or event: New Zealand has many local festivals and events, which are a great way to experience the country like a local. To learn more about the country and its culture, try to visit a local festival or event, such as the Matariki Festival, the Auckland Lantern Festival, or the Wellington International Jazz Festival.

Hike a local trail: New Zealand is a great place for hiking, and there are many local trails to explore. To experience the best of what the country has to offer, try to hike a local trail, such as the Abel Tasman Coast Track, the Tongariro Alpine Crossing, or the Kepler Track.

Drink local beer or wine: New Zealand has a thriving craft beer and wine industry, and there are many local brews and vintages to try. To experience the best of what the country has to offer, try to drink some local beer or wine, such as a pint of Tuatara Brew or a glass of Marlborough Sauvignon Blanc.

Overall, with some local knowledge, transport, and activities, you can experience the best of what New Zealand has to offer as a local. Whether you're looking for beautiful scenery, outdoor adventure, or cultural experiences, there are many options to choose from in New Zealand.

The best time of year to visit

The best time of year to visit New Zealand depends on your personal preferences and interests. Here is some information that can help you decide when to visit New Zealand:

Peak season: The peak season in New Zealand is during the summer months of December, January, and February. During this time, the weather is warm and sunny, and many outdoor activities and attractions are available. However, the peak season is also the busiest time of year, and prices for accommodation and activities can be higher.

Shoulder season: The shoulder season in New Zealand is during the spring and fall months of September, October, November, March, and April. During this time, the weather is mild and pleasant, and there are fewer crowds and lower prices than during the peak season. However, some outdoor activities and attractions may be closed or have limited availability during the shoulder season.

Off-season: The off-season in New Zealand is during the winter months of May, June, July, and August. During this time, the weather can be cold and wet, and some outdoor activities and attractions may be closed or have limited availability. However, the off-season is also the least busy time of year, and prices for accommodation and activities can be lower.

Overall, the best time of year to visit New Zealand depends on your personal preferences and interests. If you want warm weather and many outdoor activities, the peak season may be the best time for you to visit. If you want mild weather and fewer crowds, the shoulder season may be the best time for you to visit. If you want lower prices and fewer crowds, the off-season may be the best time for you to visit.

How to get around the country

There are many ways to get around New Zealand, and the best option for you will depend on your personal preferences and itinerary. Here are some options for getting around the country:

Car rental: Renting a car is a popular and convenient way to get around New Zealand. Renting a car will give you the freedom and flexibility to explore the country at your own pace, and you can visit remote and less-visited areas that are not accessible by public transport. However, renting a car can be expensive, and it's important to be aware of the country's strict driving rules and road conditions.

Bus and coach: Taking a bus or coach is a cost-effective and convenient way to get around New Zealand. Buses and coaches are available throughout the country, and they can take you to many popular destinations. Buses and coaches are also a great way to meet other travelers and learn more about the country. However, bus and coach travel can be time-consuming, and schedules and routes may be limited.

Train: Taking a train is a scenic and comfortable way to get around New Zealand. Trains are available on the North and South Islands, and they can take you to many popular destinations. Taking a train is a great way to relax and enjoy the beautiful scenery of the country, and it's also a good option if you have limited mobility. However, trains can be expensive, and schedules and routes may be limited.

Air: Flying is a fast and convenient way to get around New Zealand. There are many domestic flights available throughout the country, and they can take you to many popular destinations. Flying is a great option if you have a tight schedule or want to visit remote areas, and it's also a good option if you have a lot of luggage. However, flying can be expensive, and it's not a good option if you want to experience the beautiful scenery of the country.

Overall, there are many options for getting around New Zealand, and the best option for you will depend on your personal preferences and itinerary. Whether you want freedom and flexibility, cost-effectiveness, comfort, or speed, there's an option for you in New Zealand.

Local customs and etiquette

New Zealand is a friendly and welcoming country, and there are some local customs and etiquette that you should be aware of when you visit. Here are some tips for respecting local customs and etiquette in New Zealand:

Greeting people: In New Zealand, it's customary to greet people with a handshake, a smile, and direct eye contact. If you're unsure how to greet someone, it's best to wait for them to initiate the greeting.

Saying thank you: In New Zealand, it's customary to say "thank you" (or "thanks") to show appreciation and gratitude. Saying thank you is important in many situations, such as when someone gives you something, helps you, or provides you with a service.

Gift-giving: In New Zealand, gift-giving is not as common or expected as it is in some other countries. If you're invited to someone's home, it's polite to bring a small gift, such as a bottle of wine, a box of chocolates, or a bouquet of flowers. However, it's not necessary to bring a gift, and it's important not to overdo it or make a big fuss.

Table manners: In New Zealand, table manners are similar to those in many other Western countries. It's polite to use utensils to eat, to keep your elbows off the table, and to say "please" and "thank you" when you ask for something or are served. It's also polite to wait for everyone to be seated and served before starting to eat and to wait for the host to signal that it's okay to leave the table.

Maori culture: In New Zealand, the Maori culture is an important part of the country's heritage and identity. To show respect and appreciation for the Maori culture, it's important to be aware of and follow some basic customs, such as removing your shoes when entering a Maori home or marae (meeting ground), and standing when a Karanga (call) is made by a woman. It's also important to avoid using the Maori language or cultural symbols without permission.

In addition to the customs and etiquette mentioned above, there are some other local customs and etiquette that you should be aware of when you visit New Zealand. Here are some more tips for respecting local customs and etiquette in New Zealand:

Tipping: In New Zealand, tipping is not as common or expected as it is in some other countries. Tipping is generally not required in restaurants, cafes, or bars, and it's not necessary to tip taxi drivers, hairdressers, or other service providers. However, if you receive exceptional service, it's acceptable to leave a small tip, such as 10% of the total bill, as a gesture of appreciation.

Smoking: In New Zealand, smoking is not as common or accepted as it is in some other countries. Smoking is prohibited in many public places, such as restaurants, bars, cafes, and public buildings, and it's also illegal to smoke in some outdoor areas, such as playgrounds, sports fields, and public parks. If you want to smoke, it's important to look for designated smoking areas and to dispose of your cigarette butts responsibly.

Littering: In New Zealand, litter is considered a serious offense, and it's important to avoid litter. Littering is prohibited in many public places, and it's also illegal to leave litter in some outdoor areas, such as national parks, forests, and beaches. If you want to dispose of litter, it's important to look for designated litter bins, and to follow the "Leave No Trace" principles.

Alcohol: In New Zealand, alcohol is widely available and consumed, and it's important to be aware of and follow some basic rules and guidelines. It's illegal to purchase or consume alcohol if you're under the age of 18, and it's also illegal to drink alcohol in public places, such as streets, parks, and beaches. If you want to drink alcohol, it's important to do so responsibly and to avoid driving or operating machinery while under the influence.

New Zealand is a friendly and welcoming country, and it's important to respect local customs and etiquette when you visit. By following these tips, you can show respect and appreciation for the country's culture and people, and you can have a more enjoyable and rewarding experience in New Zealand.

Where to find the best deals and discounts

There are many ways to find the best deals and discounts in New Zealand, and the best option for you will depend on your personal preferences and itinerary. Here are some tips for finding the best deals and discounts in New Zealand:

Online: Online platforms, such as booking websites, travel agencies, and social media groups, are great places to find the best deals and discounts in New Zealand. Online platforms often offer special discounts and promotions, and they can also provide valuable information and reviews about the products and services that you're interested in. To find the best deals and discounts online, try to compare prices and packages, and read reviews and ratings from other travelers.

In-person: In person, there are many places where you can find the best deals and discounts in New Zealand. For example, you can visit local visitor centers, travel agencies, and tourism offices, and you can ask for information and advice about the best deals and discounts in the area. You can also visit local shops, restaurants, and attractions, and you can ask for special offers and discounts. To find the best deals and discounts in person, try to be friendly and polite, and be flexible and open-minded.

Special offers: Special offers are a great way to find the best deals and discounts in New Zealand. Special offers are often available during the off-season, or during special events, such as public holidays, festivals, and concerts. Special offers can include discounts on accommodation, activities, food, and transportation, and they can provide great value for money. To find the best special offers, try to look for information and updates on the websites and social media accounts of the companies and organizations that you're interested in.

Loyalty programs: Loyalty programs are another way to find the best deals and discounts in New Zealand. Loyalty programs are offered by many companies and organizations, and they can provide rewards and benefits to customers who are loyal and frequent. Loyalty programs can include discounts, points, rewards, and perks, and they can provide great value for money. To find the best loyalty programs, try to look for information and updates on the websites and social media accounts of the companies and organizations that you're interested in.

There are many ways to find the best deals and discounts in New Zealand, and the best option for you will depend on your personal preferences and itinerary. By looking online, in person, and for special offers and loyalty programs, you can find the best deals and discounts in New Zealand and save money on your trip.

Robyn Russel

Chapter 10: Why New Zealand is a must-visit destination

New Zealand is a must-visit destination for many reasons. Here are some of the reasons why New Zealand is a must-visit destination:

Natural beauty: New Zealand is known for its stunning natural beauty, and it's a paradise for nature lovers and outdoor enthusiasts. The country has a diverse landscape, ranging from mountains, forests, and lakes, to beaches, fjords, and islands. New Zealand is also home to many unique and endangered species of plants and animals, such as the kiwi bird, the tuatara reptile, and the kauri tree.

Adventure sports: New Zealand is a great destination for adventure sports and outdoor activities, and it offers many opportunities for thrill-seekers and adrenaline junkies. The country has many natural attractions and landmarks, such as glaciers, waterfalls, and volcanoes, and it offers many adventure sports, such as bungee jumping, skydiving, rafting, and hiking. New Zealand is also home to many adventure sports companies and organizations, which provide professional and safe services for travelers.

Cultural heritage: New Zealand has a rich and diverse cultural heritage, and it's a great destination for cultural exploration and discovery. The country has two main cultures, the Maori and the Europeans, and it's a melting pot of many other cultures, such as Asian, Pacific, and Middle Eastern. New Zealand is also home to many cultural attractions and events, such as museums, galleries, and festivals, which provide insight and understanding into the country's history and traditions.

Food and drink: New Zealand is a great destination for food and drinks lovers, and it offers many delicious and unique culinary experiences. The country has a diverse and thriving food and drink industry, which combines local ingredients, such as seafood, lamb, and dairy, with global flavors and techniques. New Zealand is also home to many wineries, breweries, and distilleries, which produce high-quality and award-winning wines, beers, and spirits.

Overall, New Zealand is a must-visit destination for many reasons, including its natural beauty, adventure sports, cultural heritage, and food and drink. By visiting New Zealand, you can experience the country's unique and fascinating culture, and you can have a memorable and rewarding trip.

The many reasons to visit New Zealand

New Zealand is a great destination for many reasons, and it offers many opportunities for travelers. Here are some reasons why you should go to New Zealand:

Natural beauty: New Zealand is known for its stunning natural beauty, and it's a paradise for nature lovers and outdoor enthusiasts. The country has a diverse and stunning landscape, which includes mountains, forests, lakes, beaches, fjords, and islands. The country's natural beauty is also unique and special because of its biodiversity, which includes many unique and endangered species of plants and animals, such as the kiwi bird, the tuatara reptile, and the kauri tree.

Adventure sports. New Zealand is a great destination for adventure sports and outdoor activities, and it offers many opportunities for thrill-seekers and adrenaline junkies. The country has many natural attractions and landmarks, such as glaciers, waterfalls, and volcanoes, and it offers many adventure sports, such as bungee jumping, skydiving, rafting, and hiking. New Zealand is also home to many adventure sports companies and organizations, which provide professional and safe services for travelers.

Cultural heritage: New Zealand has a rich and diverse cultural heritage, and it's a great destination for cultural exploration and discovery. The country has two main cultures, the Maori and the Europeans, and it's a melting pot of many other cultures, such as Asian, Pacific, and Middle Eastern. New Zealand is also home to many cultural attractions and events, such as museums, galleries, and festivals, which provide insight and understanding into the country's history and traditions.

Food and drink: New Zealand is a great destination for food and drinks lovers, and it offers many delicious and unique culinary experiences. The country has a diverse and thriving food and drink industry, which combines local ingredients, such as seafood, lamb, and dairy, with global flavors and techniques. New Zealand is also home to many wineries, breweries, and distilleries, which produce high-quality and award-winning wines, beers, and spirits.

Safety: New Zealand is a safe and friendly destination for travelers, and it offers a high standard of living, healthcare, and security. The country has low crime rates, and it's considered one of the safest and most peaceful countries in the world. New Zealand also has a high level of emergency services, such as police, fire, and ambulance, and it has many hospitals, clinics, and pharmacies that provide healthcare services for travelers.

In addition to the reasons mentioned above, there are many other reasons to visit New Zealand. Here are some more reasons why you should visit New Zealand:

Landscapes: New Zealand is known for its beautiful and diverse landscapes, and it offers many opportunities to explore and discover the country's natural beauty. The country has many natural attractions and landmarks, such as mountains, forests, lakes, beaches, fjords, and islands, and it also has many national parks, reserves, and conservation areas, which protect and preserve the country's unique and fragile environment. By visiting New Zealand, you can experience the country's beautiful and varied landscapes, and you can enjoy many outdoor activities, such as hiking, camping, fishing, and boating.

Wildlife: New Zealand is also a great destination for wildlife lovers and conservationists, and it offers many opportunities to see and learn about the country's unique and fascinating animals and plants. The country has many endemic and endangered species, such as the kiwi bird, the tuatara reptile, and the kauri tree, and it also has many zoos, sanctuaries, and conservation centers, which provide information and education about the country's wildlife. By visiting New Zealand, you can learn about the country's unique and fascinating wildlife, and you can support conservation efforts and initiatives.

Activities: New Zealand is a great destination for travelers who want to experience and enjoy the country's culture, history, and traditions. The country has many cultural attractions and events, such as museums, galleries, and festivals, which provide insight and understanding into the country's history, art, and music. The country also has many cultural experiences and performances, such as Maori cultural shows, which showcase the country's traditional and contemporary culture. By visiting New Zealand, you can experience and enjoy the country's culture, history, and traditions, and you can learn more about its rich and diverse heritage.

People: New Zealand is a great destination for travelers who want to meet and interact with the country's friendly and welcoming people. The country has a diverse and multicultural population, which includes Maori, European, Asian, Pacific, and Middle Eastern communities, and it has a reputation for being a friendly and hospitable country. By visiting New Zealand, you can meet and interact with the country's people, and you can learn more about their culture, history, and traditions.

There are many reasons to visit New Zealand, and the country offers many opportunities for travelers to experience and enjoy its unique and fascinating culture, history, and people. By visiting New Zealand, you can have a memorable and rewarding trip, and you can learn more about the country's beauty, wildlife, activities, and people.

How to make the most of your trip to New Zealand

To make the most of your trip to New Zealand, there are several things you can do. Here are some tips for making the most of your trip to New Zealand:

Plan ahead: Before you visit New Zealand, it's important to plan your trip carefully. Research the country's attractions, activities, and events, and create an itinerary that includes the things you want to see and do. Also, plan your transportation, accommodation, and budget, and consider any special needs or requirements you may have, such as visas, insurance, or medical care. By planning ahead, you can ensure that your trip to New Zealand is smooth, enjoyable, and stress-free.

Be flexible: New Zealand is a large and diverse country, and it offers many opportunities for exploration and discovery. To make the most of your trip, it's important to be flexible and open-minded and to be ready to try new things and experiences. Consider traveling to different regions and cities, and visiting different attractions and landmarks. Also, be open to local culture and customs, and try new foods, drinks, and activities. By being flexible and open-minded, you can have a richer and more rewarding trip to New Zealand.

Be respectful: New Zealand is a friendly and welcoming country, and its people are known for their hospitality and kindness. To make the most of your trip, it's important to be respectful and considerate of the country's culture, history, and people. Be polite and courteous, and follow local laws and customs. Also, be respectful of the country's natural beauty and wildlife, and follow the guidelines and rules for conservation and sustainability. By being respectful and considerate, you can have a positive and enjoyable trip to New Zealand.

Be adventurous: New Zealand is a great destination for adventure and outdoor activities, and it offers many opportunities for thrill-seekers and adrenaline junkies. To make the most of your trip, it's important to be adventurous and try new things and experiences. Consider participating in adventure sports and outdoor activities, such as bungee jumping, skydiving, rafting, and hiking. Also, be open to local culture and traditions, and try new foods, drinks, and activities. By being adventurous, you can have a fun and exciting trip to New Zealand.

To make the most of your trip to New Zealand, it's important to plan ahead, be flexible, be respectful, and be adventurous. By following these tips, you can have a memorable and rewarding trip to New Zealand, and you can experience and enjoy the country's unique and fascinating culture, history, and people.

In addition to the tips mentioned above, there are several other things you can do to make the most of your trip to New Zealand. Here are some more tips for making the most of your trip to New Zealand:

Explore: New Zealand is a large and diverse country, and it offers many opportunities for exploration and discovery. To make the most of your trip, it's important to explore the country's different regions and cities and to visit different attractions and landmarks. Consider traveling to the North Island and the South Island, and to the major cities, such as Auckland, Wellington, and Christchurch. Also, consider visiting some of the country's natural attractions and landmarks, such as mountains, forests, lakes, beaches, and fjords. By exploring the country, you can have a richer and more rewarding trip to New Zealand.

Learn: New Zealand is a great destination for learning and education, and it offers many opportunities to learn about the country's culture, history, and people. To make the most of your trip, it's important to learn about the country's culture, history, and people, and to gain insight and understanding into their traditions, customs, and art forms. Consider visiting some of the country's cultural attractions and events, such as museums, galleries, and festivals, and consider participating in some cultural experiences and performances, such as Maori cultural shows. By learning about the country, you can have a more meaningful and rewarding trip to New Zealand.

Enjoy: New Zealand is a great destination for enjoyment and relaxation, and it offers many opportunities to relax, unwind, and recharge. To make the most of your trip, it's important to enjoy the country's natural beauty and wildlife and to have fun and be entertained. Consider visiting some of the country's natural attractions and landmarks, such as mountains, forests, lakes, beaches, and fjords, and consider participating in some outdoor activities and adventure sports, such as hiking, camping, fishing, and boating. Also, consider trying some of the country's delicious and unique foods and drinks, and consider attending some of the country's cultural events and festivals. By enjoying the country, you can have a more pleasurable and satisfying trip to New Zealand.

Overall, to make the most of your trip to New Zealand, it's important to explore, learn, and enjoy the country. By following these tips, you can have a memorable and rewarding trip to New Zealand, and you can experience and appreciate the country's unique and fascinating culture, history, and people.

Tips for traveling with kids or pets

Traveling with kids or pets can add an extra level of complexity to your trip, but it can also be an incredibly rewarding experience. If you're planning a trip to New Zealand with your little ones or furry friends, here are some tips to help you make the most of your adventure.

Research child-friendly and pet-friendly accommodations. New Zealand has a wide range of accommodations to choose from, but not all of them are suitable for families or pets. Look for hotels or vacation rentals that have kid-friendly amenities like cribs or play areas and pet-friendly options like fenced yards or designated pet areas.

Plan your itinerary with their needs in mind. When traveling with kids or pets, it's important to consider their needs and interests when planning your itinerary. Look for activities and attractions that will be fun and engaging for them, and try to schedule plenty of breaks and downtime for rest and relaxation.

Pack the essentials. Make sure you have all the necessary gear and supplies for your kids or pets, including things like strollers, car seats, leashes, and food and water. It's also a good idea to bring along some familiar toys or treats to help them feel more comfortable in a new environment.

Consider hiring a local guide or babysitter. If you're worried about managing your kids or pets on your own, consider hiring a local guide or babysitter to help you out. They can provide expert advice and support, and take care of your little ones while you enjoy some adult time.

Be prepared for unexpected challenges. Traveling with kids or pets can sometimes be unpredictable, so it's important to be prepared for any challenges that might arise. Bring along a first aid kit and any necessary medications, and make sure you have a plan in case of an emergency.

Overall, traveling with kids or pets can be an incredibly rewarding experience. By following these tips and being prepared for any challenges that might come up, you can make the most of your trip to New Zealand and create lasting memories with your little ones or furry friends.

Plan for long travel days. New Zealand is a large country, and some of the best attractions are located far from the major cities. If you're planning a road trip or a long journey by plane or train, make sure you have plenty of entertainment and snacks for your kids or pets to keep them happy and comfortable.

Stay safe in the outdoors. New Zealand has some amazing outdoor experiences to offer, from hiking and biking to water sports and wildlife encounters. However, it's important to be aware of the potential hazards and take appropriate safety measures. Always follow the local advice and guidelines, and make sure your kids or pets are properly supervised at all times.

Conclusion

New Zealand is a beautiful and fascinating country, and it offers many opportunities for travelers to experience and enjoy its natural beauty, culture, history, and people. The country has a rich and diverse culture, which includes the Maori and European cultures, and it's a melting pot of many other cultures, such as Asian, Pacific, and Middle Eastern. New Zealand is also home to many natural attractions and landmarks, such as mountains, forests, lakes, beaches, and fjords, and it offers many outdoor activities and adventure sports, such as hiking, camping, fishing, and boating.

To make the most of your trip to New Zealand, it's important to plan ahead, be flexible, be respectful, and be adventurous. By following these tips, you can have a memorable and rewarding trip to New Zealand, and you can experience and enjoy the country's unique and fascinating culture, history, and people.

In conclusion, New Zealand is a great destination for travelers who want to experience and enjoy the country's natural beauty, culture, history, and people. By visiting New Zealand, you can have a memorable and rewarding trip, and you can learn more about the country's beauty, wildlife, activities, and people.

Printed in Great Britain
by Amazon